# Are You a Target?

*Fight the Good Fight*
*God's Way Workbook*

Elizabeth Hilby

Are You a Target?
Fight the Good Fight God's Way Workbook
Copyright © 2017 by Princess Writer, LLC Elizabeth Hilby
© 2019 2nd. Edition,
ISBN 978-0-9967411-2-5

Scripture references quoted from
Holy Bible, New International Version®, NIV® Copyright ©
1973, 1978, 1984, 2011 by *Biblica, Inc.*® Used by permission.
All rights reserved worldwide.
Printed in the United States, Columbia, SC
Religious / Educational / Inspirational

Author photo ©SWB Photograph (Stacey Woods Boitnott) photography
used by permission
Cover Photo: © <ahref=https://www.123rf.com/profile kagenmi> kagenmi/ 123RF stock photo used by permission.

Hand print image: www.getcoloringpages.com/coloring/20694

# Thank you

I have many friends and family who encourage my walk with God. *Thank you*, one and all!

I want to acknowledge a few,
Tammi, Bill, and Julie
*Thank you*, for introducing me to the Holy Spirit over 30 years ago and growing.

My Pastors Jerry and Denise, my Life Group leaders Angela and Johnnie, and my Life Group partner Kerry, *Thank you,* for your dedication and influence as Lights in the kingdom of God to my life.

God Bless!

# CONTENTS

# Introduction

My desire as I write this book is to put a tool in your
hand to help you recognize your authority in Christ
through his blood-bought redemption as a child of
God. This workbook is an extension of its Mother
book,

Are You a Target: Fight the Good Fight God's Way

ISBN 978-0-9967411-3-2

Published by Pen It! Publications, LLC.

I want to encourage you to take time as you learn to
battle or strengthen your sword as a prayer warrior.
Some of the questions may be uncomfortable to face; I
encourage you to do it anyway! Let God wash your
soul, will, and emotions so you can grow stronger in

Him.

Beloved, you have a battle on your hands, but you do not have anything to fear! Jesus in you is greater than anything the devil can throw your way. Many say, "The devil is cunning." *Yes, he is, but he is not greater than Jesus!* The Word of God is alive and active. It divides the deception of the enemy from Truth. It does this by separating light from darkness, sickness from health, poverty from wealth, sin from holiness, lack of forgiveness to bring forgiveness, and peace from the storm.

Jesus already won the war against sin and Satan. However, that does not mean Satan steps aside when we accept Jesus as our Savior. Quite the contrary, in this new identity in Christ, we become a target. Satan will target us personally through distorting our identity, delaying our destiny, defiling our heritage-our children, or demeaning our ability to serve in the kingdom. He knows he must disarm us before he can cripple us.

The purpose of this workbook and the partner devotional Are You a Target is to educate and equip you with God's truth concerning Spiritual Warfare. Knowledge is POWER! Beloved of God, as his child, Power is in you through the authority of the name of Jesus. Are you ready to activate it to fight and win? Let's go on a journey of discovery and building spiritual muscles together. Amen!

## *Journal About it.*

Think about what you hope to get out of this
workbook. I pray with you that by the time you finish
you can say, "Thank you, Jesus!"

# God Time

Time is Priceless. We all have 24 hours in a day to spread between family needs, work, household chores, and personal needs. We all have at least these. The list continues individually. God knows how busy we are! That is why he tells us to be in prayer and praise continually. The time of our day seems to extend if we begin with God. We can accomplish more in less time as we give him place in our lives. Plus, time spent with God develops our ears to hear and spirits to be at peace. Why?

It is typical for the activity that dominates your time to grow in strength. Look at muscle builders, athletes, and scholars to see where they spend their time. Even in the church, those who spend time with God have a stronger understanding and ministry then someone who only attends Sunday service. Productive time spent towards something reaps good rewards.

For myself, unproductive time often reaps regret or stress as I rush to do a task neglected. The business of life, as well as the lazy days of leisure, often cause my Bible or prayer time to be set aside. I plan to do it later. The problem is, *later* never comes. At least, this is my personal experience!

I want to challenge you as part of this study to commit to yourself to spend time daily in the Word of God and prayer. You can only learn to know God's guidance through time spent with him.

**EXERCISE:** Pray about committing to prayer and the Word daily.

*I commit to _____ time of worship.*

*I commit to _____ time in prayer.*

*I commit to _____ time in the Word.*

*Write a Prayer of Commitment:*

Beloved, Jesus ascended to heaven and tour down the curtain for you to meet with God at his holy throne. You do that in your prayer time. This plea is not to encourage religious rhetoric or bring conviction. It is to help you to be mindful of how much *quality* time you spend with God not necessarily to add a *quantity* of time. Amen.

Prayer is not an elusive and mystical thing. It is merely talking to the Father. Just as you and I can connect through the written words of this workbook, you and Father God can connect. The difference is, on my side, this is a monolog. I don't get to hear your answers or see your feelings. With God that is not the case. It is not you speak; he listens. It is a conversation where you both express your hearts. The key is being silent as it was with worship to allow God the opportunity to talk to you.

God speaks to each of us differently. Sometimes it is an impression in our "spirit," we just know. Sometimes it is a voice from within the pit of our belly, or it could be an intense thought that directs to do something. It could be the Word of God that suddenly jumps off the pages into your spirit that ignites a fire as you have never experienced. (This is the expression of a Rhema, revelation knowledge Word from God to you!)

**EXERCISE:** As you read your Bible, write the scriptures that belong to you; the Rhema that God ignites inside your soul and spirit.

*

*

*

*

*

*

# *Journal*
## What did God impress as you meditated?

Final note, the posture in which you approach God in prayer does not have limitations. You can sit, lay, stand, or kneel. Being obedient to the leading of the Holy Spirit with your posture is lifting a humble prayer to the Father. Talk with God as you ask a request, give thanks, and offer praise to him for what he has done. You can and should thank him *before* the answer comes! These are all prayer. Sounds simple? It is! Read Psalms for many examples of physical descriptions of prayer and worship by Moses and David.

I have had answered prayers both long-winded and short. I have many healing testimonies I share in my other books that are listed at the back with Author information. I also have needs that I long-suffer over in prayer. I know the answer will be seen on earth as it is in heaven because Jesus's sacrifice on the cross bought redemption in every area of my life. I must stand in faith to see the response manifest this side of heaven.

I know— it isn't always easy. However, even when it is not easy, or our faith feels too small, God gave us the answer we need to stand firm! It is up to us to seek it out.

One way you can do that is by praying before you read the Bible. Invite the Holy Spirit to show you where to locate your needed encouragement or guidance. He is faithful to reveal the answer. It may not be the answer you want, but it is wise to give the issue to God to have his way. Lay down your will as Jesus and say, *"Never-the-less, not my will but thine be done"* (Luke 22:42).

Pray daily, pray often, even without ceasing to bring your petition to God. When you feel the holy hush of God's presence, I encourage you to sit and wait. Maybe God will give you an answer, perhaps he will not, but you will still know the peace of his presence for strength to continue.

# *Battle of the Will*

*"I do not understand what I do. For what I want to do
I do not do, but what I hate I do. And if I do what I do
not want to do, I agree that the law is good. As it is, it
is no longer I myself who do it, but it is sin living in
me. For I know that good itself does not dwell in me,
that is, in my sinful nature. For I have the desire to do
what is good, but I cannot carry it out. For I do not do
the good I want to do, but the evil I do not want to do—
this I keep on doing. Now if I do what I do not want to
do, it is no longer I who do it, but it is sin living in me
that does it."*

Romans 7:15-20

Can you relate to Paul? I sure can!
What does Paul's exhortation stir in your spirit?

Jesus had a battle.

Read Jesus' struggle in Luke 22:39-46.

Do you see, Jesus had this same struggle as Paul, and he overcame by the Word of His Testimony?

**EXERCISE:** Think about this example as you pray about your struggles.

Do you have a chapter and verse that tells you God's answer to your struggle? If so, write out a prayer using the Word of God. Meditate on the scriptures to get your thoughts to line up with His will for you.

Pray it through until you can say,

**"Nevertheless, not my will, but Yours be done."**

## *The Interference We Face*

What thoughts control your actions?

*"A good man brings good things out of the good stored up in his heart, and an evil man brings evil things out of the evil stored up in his heart. For the mouth speaks what the heart is full of." Luke 6:45*

Beloved, thoughts will influence the heart.
Pray for the Lord to show you where your thoughts are not kingdom focused.

**EXERCISE:** Journal Holy Spirit's impression.

# *Journal*

**EXERCISE:** Search the Concordance in your Bible using the keyword: *thoughts* (or search online). Write scriptures to retrain your thinking to line up with God's plan for your life.

*

*

*

Check your heart to guard your mouth.

*"The tongue has the power of life and death, and those who love it will eat its fruit." Proverbs 18:21*

**EXERCISE:** Evaluate your speech.

Journal what the Lord shows you about your mouth.

Do my words line up or against God's Word?

Think about it as you ask:
"What catchphrase do I regularly use that is not godly?"

Old phrase:

My replacement:

Old phrase:

My replacement:

Old phrase:

My replacement:

Practice the new phrase/phrases to rewrite it/them in your heart to agree with God's word.

What we confess is what we will see become evident in our lives.

Son Shiner Speak LIFE to shine the light of Jesus!

**EXERCISE:** Look up and write out the scriptures that agree with God's Word in your areas of lack.

For example:
The lack: A broken body, sickness.
The answer: *I Am Healed by Jesus's Stripes!*

Your turn
The lack:


The answer:


The lack:


The answer:


The lack:


The answer:


The lack:

The answer:

# *Know the Voice of God*

*"Therefore, there is now no condemnation for those who are in Christ Jesus, because through Christ Jesus the law of the Spirit who gives life has set you free from the law of sin and death. For what the law was powerless to do because it was weakened by the flesh, God did by sending his own Son in the likeness of sinful flesh to be a sin offering. And so he condemned sin in the flesh, in order that the righteous requirement of the law might be fully met in us, who do not live according to the flesh but according to the Spirit."*
Romans 8:1-4, NIV

Guilt is not of God. Neither is condemnation that makes you feel bad about yourself. It is a direct contrast to a conviction which leads to repentance and draws you to Jesus. Jesus took sin and nailed it to the cross. That included condemnation and shame. Amen

Conviction is a good thing. It is God's way of revealing little or big habits, temptations, or transgressions hidden in the deep crevasses of the spirit. They must go in Jesus name! They are open doors for the devil to have access to meddle in your and your children's lives.

As you participate in the inward seeking exercise, it may stir some past thoughts or sin you had conquered. First, ask God "Have I truly put this under the blood?" If so, recognize this is the enemy who wants to get you down! He wants to stop your progress forward as a prayer warrior with power and faith to stand against his trickery and deceit. Rebuke the liar and declare your freedom in this area. Amen! If not, give it to God as you pray through until *He* gives you release as you include them in the following exercise.

**EXERCISE:** Journal about any areas of guilt. Bring them to the LIGHT to release their hold on you.

Now tear up the debt whether it is your own or someone else's. Since the blood of Jesus cleansed you from guilt, plead the blood of Jesus over those areas and throw them into the sea of forgetfulness. God does not hold them against you, and neither should you! Amen! Be Free by the Blood of the Lamb and the word of your testimony.

**EXERCISE:** Read Luke 22:31-34, 55-62

Peter was convicted when he heard that rooster crow; he remembered the warning Jesus gave him that Satan would try to sift him. Peter also remembered Jesus' warning that he (Peter) would deny him (Jesus) three times. Peter heard that rooster, and it all came crashing in. Peter repented in tears when conviction hit. I image convicts that brought tears turned into condemnation that whispered in Peter's ear, "You swore you would not deny him, and you did; not once, but multiple times! Jesus will not forgive you. You're not his friend!"

After Jesus returned from the grave, he told the woman go tell *"His disciples and Peter"*

*"I go ahead of them to Galilee"* (Mark 16:7).
Jesus called out Peter to let him know it was okay.
He knew Peter's heart and anguish. Jesus knew
Peter needed affirmation. Peter heard the
invitation of his LORD and did not let
condemnation keep him away. He ran to his
Savior!

After the Holy Spirit filled him, Peter
stood boldly and proclaimed Jesus, the Savior,
who died, arose, and sat at the right hand of the
Father. He was now who God destined him to be,
a voice for his glory!

Conviction is not pleasant, but it is a loving
reminder from God we may have his nature, but we
still contend with the flesh. Our flesh should be
subdued to submit to the Spirit. That is the only way to
live the life that fulfills our call. Amen.

If you realized an area of conviction from Holy
Spirit that needs cleansing, praise God for his

revelation knowledge! Pray about whom you can go to for help or Christian accountability if necessary.


**EXERCISE:** Remember whose nature you have. Meditate on these to get your self-image in agreement.

Ephesians 4:24


Colossians 3:1-12


2 Corinthians 5:17


Your turn. Whose nature do you imitate? Find the scripture and write them here for a point of reference in your time of need.

*

*

*

*

*

\*

\*

\*

\*

# Journal about it.

# *Temptations We Face*

Beloved, God does not tempt us with evil!

Jesus taught us to pray against temptations in Matthew 6 in the Lord's Prayer. He prayed, *"Lead us not into temptation..."* God even tells us to flee evil when it comes to sexual temptations. He does not want us to stand around and see if we can handle it. Sexual attraction is the only time the Bible tells us to RUN~! (1 Corinthians 6:18)

We all struggle with some form of sin. Gossip, lying, worry, theft, a bad attitude, anger, the list could go on and on. What we do when the desire strikes to do something against God's word is the difference between sin and holy living. How we respond to the voice in our head as soon as it whispers, sets us up to stand or fall. The whisper is not our moment of sin, the action that bends to it is.

**EXERCISE:** Recognize thoughts of temptation.

My temptation is: _____

Do a word search to find a verse to help you stand.

Write the reference and pray it.

*

*

*

Lay it out before God and ask Holy Spirit for a plan to help you conquer that mountain once and for all!

Temptation: _____

Plan to overcome:

Temptation:_____

Plan to overcome:

# *Practice God's Presence*

*"Sing to the LORD, all the earth; proclaim his salvation day after day. Declare his glory among the nations, his marvelous deeds among all peoples. For great is the LORD and most worthy of praise; he is to be feared above all gods. For all the gods of the nations are idols, but the LORD made the heavens. Splendor and majesty are before him; strength and joy are in his dwelling place. Ascribe to the LORD, all you families of nations, ascribe to the LORD glory and strength. Ascribe to the LORD the glory due his name; bring an offering and come before him.*

*Worship the LORD in the splendor of his holiness.*

*Tremble before him, all the earth! The world is firmly*

*established; it cannot be moved. Let the heavens*

*rejoice, let the earth be glad; let them say among the*

*nations, "The LORD reigns!"*

1 Chronicles 16:23-31

Worship brings us into the presence of God. It invites him to speak to us and brings peace. As you read the above text, did you get a renewed *awe* of the majesty and splendor of the God we serve? The Father of all creation loves you and me and wants to have an audience with us! Isn't that amazing? I am both awestruck and humbled that my God wants to meet with me! He desires to meet with you just as much! He waits for your times of praise and worship.

Consider, worship and praise do a few things.

* They invite the presence of God to come.
* They lift you up.
* They put your gaze on the right focus.
* They bring a spirit of peace and joy.
* It is obedient; obedience brings blessings.
* Worries fade in the wake of worship.
* God is glorified on earth and demon's tremble!

Worship washes away the dirt, clutter, and distractions so you can see what is most important. Worship ushers you into the throne room of God behind the curtain that held the Israelites at bay. As a blood-bought child of the Most-High God, you *"Get to"* meet with **Him** in the Holy of Holies daily. Even multiple times daily if you need/want to! God does not put a restraint on how often you come in worship, praise, or prayer.

*"Rejoice always, pray continually, give thanks in all circumstances; for this is God's will for you in Christ Jesus."* 1 Thessalonians 5:16-17

**EXERCISE:** Worship God in a new way.

Raise your hands in surrender, bow your head humbly, dance as you rejoice in His goodness. The way you cheer for your favorite sport's team— that is the way you can praise with excitement to God.

Perhaps you have never worshipped to the point of feeling His Presence. Today is a good day to start. Put on your favorite worship music. (YouTube has many artists that can usher in God's presence.) Put all distractions aside and take the time necessary to break through the cares or worry and simply love God.

Think of it as a date with your Groom, Jesus, or a special time with your Father. Identifying with Jesus and God through the Holy Spirit in this way will help you to praise confidently and relieve the stress that captivates your thoughts.

It is only by the presence of Holy Spirit that you can meet with God the Father through Jesus, the Son. They are three in agreement. As you lift worship, it will also fill your ears, heart, soul, and spirit to bring you into a oneness of Spirit with God. As part of the worship, acknowledge God's love and your dependence on his love.

**EXERCISE:** Look up scripture on worship. Write those references here for future use.

*

*

*

*

After a time of worship and meditation before God, sit quietly as the music plays.

Silence honors God by giving him time to speak. Somedays all I do is sit quietly. God does not talk, and neither do I. I just relax as worship washes over me. I think of his love and goodness towards me. For me, this is the most intimate time spent with Jesus.

It compares to a date with the one you love. You enjoy one another's presence. You may look at one another and smile, but no words need be spoken. It is a sweet time of intimacy, isn't it? It feels satisfying even though nothing happened; it was a precious moment together.

There can be times of worship like that. You smile, God smiles, but no one speaks. Just because nothing was said does not mean nothing happened! I believe when we sit and wait, we show God our trust and he moves on those things that weigh us down without us saying a word.

You may not have an earthly Father to talk to anymore; I don't. But you always have a heavenly Father ready to hear you.

You may not have a natural husband to talk to or you may but cannot speak with him about spiritual needs. You do have Jesus who calls you his Bride! He is your spiritual husband that prays for you daily and waits to hear from you.

**EXERCISE:** Find verse about who you are to God.

*

*

*

*

*

Ask God to speak to you.

Then, WAIT FOR HIM TO SPEAK…

Give God your ear to hear. Often, we finish our list and time is up. We forget to wait and see if God has something to say. Remember the old saying, *"You have two ears to hear and one mouth to speak."* His design could be God's way of letting us know to listen to hear more than we open our mouth to speak.

**EXERCISE:** Find scriptures that minister to you about hearing God's voice. Write them, then recite them to him.

*

*

*

*

Practice hearing from God. It could be through reading scripture, a song, a phone call, or sitting quiet and a word is impressed in your thoughts.

**Journal about it.**

# *Your Mission*

I did a teaching on *Discovering your calling from God*. In it, each participant looked at their life as a puzzle being put together by God. I include this exercise for you to look at your life to see what has been the thread that is forever present. As you think about your life to this point, what are the things that have been consistent from childhood, through the teen years, and followed you into your adult life? That is the key to finding God's call if you do not yet know.

For instance, I have always enjoyed writing. As a child, I wrote stories and drew the pictures to make color/story books that I then read to my younger sisters. I wrote poetry throughout my Jr High and High School years. I even wrote a gossip column!

As an adult, I created the workbooks I taught at a preschool where I worked. Did I know God was prepping me to start a writing career over 50 years of age? No, I did not. However, the desire and interest were always there as was the passion and heart to help others who struggle or have a hard life.

Another thread, strangers have always told me their life's history. My kids asked me often "Why do people tell you their problems?" My answer,

"Because they sense the presence of God in me." That was true, but a call to counsel was also being birthed. I earned my degree in Christian Counseling at age 60! I am proof you are never too old to walk in your destiny.

That said, let's get to work on your life's puzzle to see if you can pinpoint a call or ministry God has built inside your *DNA: Designated Natural Ability* to do the work God predestined for you. Destiny is your portion. Before you were formed in your mother's womb, God put it in you. That is true even when you do not know your parents.

Every event of your life good, bad, or ugly played a part in creating who you are today. The heartache you experienced could be the pointing finger to your ministry. The trials, celebrations, and jobs all influence the discovering of your destiny. Also, add hobbies, interest, or ministry that flows smoothly. These are

44

perhaps things that will point to a call you have yet to embrace fully. Usually, God does not suddenly call us to a place that we have had no inclination or exposure. It is something embedded within.

**EXERCISE:** Use the space to organize your thoughts. Then you can place them in the hand puzzle frame.

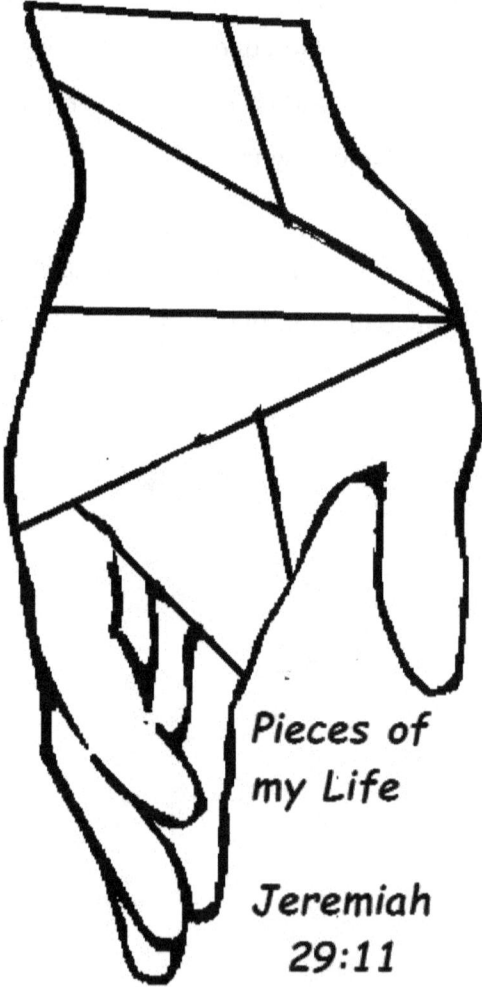

Pieces of
my Life

Jeremiah
29:11

THE PUZZLE GOD HAND CREATED
WITH MY LIFE.

## *Journal*

When you are ready, write what the LORD shows you about His plans for your future. Let God minister His plan/plans for you.

# Journal

**EXERCISE:** Find out what the Bible says about your ministry. Write the scriptures with your impressions from God. Now, meditate on them to help you to develop that area.

# *Battleground Deliverance*

Are you under attack? Probably, especially if you are doing this teaching. (I can identify. As I write this teaching, I have been on a vicious battlefield.) I describe an *attack* as *one thing after the other going wrong*. It is a constant battle to try to get above water either in health, finances, or family issues.

It is a narrow path we walk who are followers of Jesus. Jesus never sinned, and Satan tried to tempt and attack him! Just think how much more we are susceptible to his attacks! Being defensive against sin can limit Satan's ability to interfere in our lives and that of our family.

We can blindly swing our sword at the enemy or wait for God to give us discernment. Seeking God for knowledge and wisdom will provide the information we need to have eyes to see, ears to hear, and a heart to perceive how to move forward.

Knowledge is information; it puts a name to the issue. Wisdom knows how to use that information. Wisdom tells you what to do with the identified name. God will direct you to correctly apply the knowledge he shows to bring change. Amen!

We will look at two types of attacks: the legal and illegal. Attacks are *not* always because of sin. Jesus made that clear in John 9:3, *"Neither this man nor his parents sinned," said Jesus, "but this happened so that the works of God might be displayed in him."* Job is another example of a man justified by God but attacked by Satan. In both cases, men pointed with a judgmental finger and said, "Condemned," but that was not the case. It was illegal attacks God worked for good. It was Satan looking for an opportunity to attempt to stop believers from moving forward or doing God's plan with their lives.

We also have testimony in the Word that shows sin was the avenue of attacks. The woman caught in adultery was due to pay the penalty for her transgression, but Jesus stepped in on her behalf and said, *"...Let any one of you who is without sin be the first to throw a stone at her..."* (John 8:7). When all accusers left, "He gently told her, *"Go now and leave your life of sin"* (John 8:11). She deserved the stoning but there was a man from Galilee who came to set sinners free, and *He did.*

Another testimony found in John 5 tells of an invalid who lay for 38 years near the Sheep Gate pool waiting for his healing. Jesus saw him. He told him to take up his mat and walk. The man did. (The religious were angry he carried his mat on the Sabbath. But that is a whole other teaching you can study.) *"Later Jesus found him at the temple and said to him, "See, you are well again. Stop sinning, or something worse may happen to you"* (John 5:14). His sin caused the infirmity in his body. Jesus gave him deliverance from the sickness he suffered with for 38 years!

I believe Jesus tells us it was sin in scripture, so we understand sin has a penalty! It is an open door for the enemy to set his mark of attack! It was a legal attack. If we sin after becoming a believer, Satan can gain legal access through that sin to target our body, life, ministry, family, and finances.

Once forgiven we have a responsibility to "Go, sin no more." God empowers us to live a holy life set apart for His glory through grace and the Holy Spirit. (Read Titus 2:12, Hebrews 12:28.)

The Pharisees wanted a "sign" from Jesus. He got angry with them. The witness of *Who* he was, was already evident by the number of miracles he had done. Jesus answered,

*"… When an impure spirit comes out of a person, it goes through arid places seeking rest and does not find it. Then it says, 'I will return to the house I left.' When it arrives, it finds the house unoccupied, swept clean and put in order. Then it goes and takes with it seven other spirits more wicked than itself, and they go in and live there. And the final condition of that person is worse than the first. That is how it will be with this wicked generation."* Matthew 12:43-45

In this verse, Jesus tells them it is demonic spirits that take residence inside the person. I would say that is under attack, wouldn't you? So much so, that person becomes a pawn for the devil and his principalities.

Repented sin must be followed by a change in our mind, heart, and actions. We become what we think. The mind influences the heart. The heart brings changed actions. To repent of sin and then go back to doing the same thing leaves one open for more attack.

Repentance without a changed life is not repentance at all. It is an open door for more demons to invade. It is a way for the enemy to steal, kill, and destroy what Jesus wants to do in you.

I say this, not to speak condemnation or fear but to raise a warning flag. If you have asked Jesus into your heart as Lord and Savior, you cannot continue to live like the world. Christians stand apart! We are lights in the darkness. We have the nature of God within us at our re-birth.

**EXERCISE:** Study the life of someone you respect in the Word. Notice the trials or temptations they went through.

Journal about how they overcame.

## *Now Journal*

How can this knowledge help you to overcome?

Beloved, I encourage you to do what the word says. Not in a religious way, but relationally. Let this be your hearts cry, "I am one with God, and I live to please him." In living for God, you will still have attacks, but the Bible has an assurance:

*"Finally, all of you, be like-minded, be sympathetic, love one another, be compassionate and humble. Do not repay evil with evil or insult with insult. On the contrary, repay evil with blessing, because to this you were called so that you may inherit a blessing. For,*

*"Whoever would love life*
*and see good days must keep their tongue from evil*
*and their lips from deceitful speech.*
*They must turn from evil and do good;*
*they must seek peace and pursue it.*
*For the eyes of the Lord are on the righteous*
*and his ears are attentive to their prayer,*
*but the face of the Lord is against those who do evil."*

*Who is going to harm you if you are eager to do good? But even if you should suffer for what is right, you are blessed." ... "For it is better, if it is God's will, to suffer for doing good than for doing evil. For Christ also suffered once for sins, the righteous for the unrighteous, to bring you to God. He was put to death in the body but made alive in the Spirit. After being made alive, he went and made proclamation to the imprisoned spirits—to those who were disobedient long ago when God waited patiently in the days of Noah while the ark was being built. In it only a few people, eight in all, were saved through water, and this water symbolizes baptism that now saves you also—not the removal of dirt from the body but the pledge of a clear conscience toward God." It saves you by the resurrection of Jesus Christ, who has gone into heaven and is at God's right hand—with angels, authorities and powers in submission to him."*

1 Peter 3:8-13, 17-22 Amen!

**EXERCISE:** If trials fill your life, my first suggestion is to pray for discernment on whether the enemy of God has a legal ground (or not) to attack you.

What do you do once you know?

If the attack is an illegal one against you, declare the Promises in the Word that belongs to You! Remember, you are the beloved of God. Jesus paid the price for your sins; you are forgiven and free. You may need to remind yourself and the devil of this fact. Get your eyes on Jesus; stand behind the cross and let Jesus fight for you. Amen. When you have done all to do, stand with the armor of God in place. (We will look at the armor soon.) Worship God from your sorrow, this is sacrificial worship that is music to God's ears as you put your trust and faith in *Him*.

I've been through a couple of battles that the only thing I could do was worship. I felt too weak to fight.

That is when fellow believers come to the rescue!

You can even pray and ask God to have others pray as you praise. I have testimonies of my victory from standing in just that place. God came through for his glory to shine in and through my life. He will do the same for you!

If it is a legal attack by an open door of sin:

- Close the door.

    Repent to God.

    Forgive if needed.

    Ask for forgiveness if needed.

    Stop behaviors that give the devil access.

    Then you can:

- Stand in God's authority over the powers and principalities as you speak the Word of God.
- Get dressed in your spiritual armor.
- Lift the shield to stop the fiery arrows.

Once you have repented and turned from that sin and towards God, the sin is forgiven and thrown into the sea of forgetfulness. Remember Satan will try to bring condemnation to rob you of the peace Jesus bought for you to have at the cross, but we have an assurance, *"... Peace be still ..."* Mark 4:39

**EXERCISE:** Read the following references.

Write them out to help seal the word in your spirit.

2 Corinthians 12:9

Psalms 91:4

Hebrews 13:5

Hebrews 12:2

Philippians 3:1

Now, write out some faith statements to stand in the battle.

Here's a few to get started.

- I am who God says I am! My identity is in him.
- I am not a people pleaser. I am a God pleaser, first!
- I am the head and not the tail; nothing is missing or broken in my life. (Deuteronomy 28:13)
- Satan is under my feet in Jesus name! (Romans 16:20).

**EXERCISE:** Journal about God's saving grace to help you stand in victory with this wisdom and knowledge he has shown you.

# *Identity in Christ*

Read Hebrews 11 for examples of Faith-filled men and woman of the Word. How can their models of faith help you to stand?

**EXERCISE:** Notice the similarities of:

Their confessions:_____

Their devotion time:_____

What does this stir you to change?


**EXERCISE:** According to these verses, write who you are in Christ.

Romans 12:1-2

John 8:31-32

Romans 8:38-39

Identify your Fruit as His child.

1 Corinthians 13:4-7

Galatians 5:22-23

# *Journal*

My Identity in Christ is who God says I am, not what I
do.  Journal about who you see yourself as through
God's eyes. God's eyes are key here.

# *The Armor of God*

*"Finally, be strong in the Lord and in his mighty power. Put on the full armor of God, so that you can take your stand against the devil's schemes. For our struggle is not against flesh and blood, but against the rulers, against the authorities, against the powers of this dark world and against the spiritual forces of evil in the heavenly realms. Therefore put on the full armor of God, so that when the day of evil comes, you may be able to stand your ground, and after you have done everything, to stand."*
Ephesians 6:10-13

How do you dress for spiritual battle? Paul tells us:

*"Stand firm then, with the belt of truth buckled around your waist, with the breastplate of righteousness in place, and with your feet fitted with the readiness that comes from the gospel of peace. In addition to all this, take up the shield of faith, with which you can*

66

*extinguish all the flaming arrows of the evil one. Take the helmet of salvation and the sword of the Spirit, which is the word of God. And pray in the Spirit on all occasions with all kinds of prayers and requests..."*

Ephesians 6:14-18

Beloved, are you dressed? Completely?

**EXERCISE:** List the armor (Ephesians 6:14-18).

1

2

3

4

5

6

**EXERCISE**: Write how you can apply it to your life. For example, you are angry with someone. Instead of speaking from anger as you may be tempted to do, ask God to give you peace.

Forgive beforehand, put peace on your feet before you confront them.

Cover your thoughts with the helmet of salvation.

Apply the shield of faith to your heart and emotions.

Then speak to the person letting Truth guide you.

Your turn:

## Commit to dress daily to stand in battle.

*Pray, "Help me, Jesus! Thank you, Father, for loving me and calling me a child. I trust you with my whole life. In Jesus name, I commit to putting on the armor you provided.*

**EXERCISE:** List a prayer for each part of the armor as you apply it. Let Holy Spirit help you. For example, "I put on the helmet to cover my thoughts. I put on the breastplate of righteousness to cover my heart to live rightly with men and God."

1.


2.

3.

4.

5.

6

# *Journal*

What have you learned about fighting Satan through this exercise?

## Communion, the Power of the Blood

*"and when he had given thanks, he broke it and said, "This is my body, which is for you; do this in remembrance of me." In the same way, after supper he took the cup, saying, "This cup is the new covenant in my blood; do this, whenever you drink it, in remembrance of me."*

1 Corinthians 11:24–25

Consider, when Jesus instituted this rite, he was sin free. In communion, he broke his body symbolically and poured out his blood symbolically, while he was still in a state of total holiness.

The blood of Jesus is another weapon of warfare. Jesus was saying, *"My one sacrifice is all you need; now remember I Am the Bread of Life. Eat of me. I Am the blood sacrifice; drink and remember. I Am the Mediator that sits on the throne who daily intercedes for you."* (Author's inference.)

The perfection of his life lived is the perfection of our hope today. It is this perfection we eat of and drink of in faith we have access to come before the Father freely. I come when I need to, more than that when I want to. The best thing is I "get to" go to him by the body and through the blood! Halleluiah!"

"Beloved, get some juice and a cracker or piece of bread. Begin with a time of worship. Thank Jesus for all he has done on your behalf, for spiritual awakening and spiritual life renewal.

Read the words he spoke to the disciples gathered with him as you take and eat.

Pause, take time to thank him for what this means to you as his body was broken; eat, and be refreshed.

Take the cup of juice, read the words he spoke, thank him for his blood and what it means to you. Remember his bloody, ripped body, drink of this untainted blood. Now, declare the benefits that came from the cross.

Proclaim whole house salvation because of the blood.

Declare your body is whole and healthy, nothing missing, nothing broken because of this perfect body and blood that bore the pain of sin and sickness for you.

Declare fulfillment of what you lack by the blood and drink in remembrance. As you continue to do this, God will bless this time you share together to strengthen your understanding of this covenant you entered.

The battles we encounter are a place of conflict. When we pray in this manner, we aren't asking for God to do a new thing. We are calling forth our victory here on earth as God already sealed complete in heaven. We don't pray or take communion as a ploy to get God to move. We pray remembering Jesus's victory over the assailants by the blood that ran from his veins. This heart *attitude* elevates our *altitude* in Christ as we wholeheartedly remember. Thank God, we don't have to shed blood any longer. Rather than taking life as an offering, we offer our lives in thanksgiving for the blood that paid our sin debt.

Knowing his blood was for us, Jesus said fear not. Faith is the opposite of fear. When we fear, it brings a response to run away or take flight, making us easy prey. Faith stands and fights for what Jesus already won."

Excerpted from pages 224-226, Audience of One at the Mercy Seat: A Place of Prayer and Intimacy with God.

# *Journal*

Record what God speaks to you as you share the Bread
and Blood in remembrance.

# Are You A Target?

# *Resource Section*

You are the Beloved because of *Song of Solomon 2:16*, "My Beloved is mine, and I am His!"

Declare with all your heart: I believe that Jesus Christ of Nazareth was crucified, and God raised him from the dead. Now He sits on the throne at the right hand of God making intercession for me!

John 16:23 (Jesus speaking) "most assuredly I say whatever you ask the Father in My name He will give it to you." Father, I ask in Jesus name my request for _____. I know it will be done as Jesus said according to your will that my joy is full.

I thank you, Father that soon *You* will crush Satan under my feet! I've sowed in tears and my joy comes in the morning! In Jesus name I pray, Amen. (Romans 16:20, Psalms 30:5)

Those are for you. The next pages are resources you can share with fellow brothers and sisters in the Lord to encourage them on their journey. You have permission to copy them or post on Social Media. Where a copyright is listed, please include this with the material. Thank you!

## *Holy Hush*

As one waits at the throne of Almighty God

There is a holy hush that ushers in His presence.

In the turmoil of storms that batter and bang,

When the sounds are so loud, it is hard to stand,

Let the storms beat as they may.

As you sit, in a holy hush.

His presence is there to sustain you, so stay.

As the winds bellow and waves crash in:

One after another without ceasing vengeance,

Lay in His presence, prostrate on your face.

The winds will pass over, and the crashing cease

As you rest in the holy hush, all around is peace.

In the secret place of rest relief

Covered by a love that will never cease—

Be one with your Lord in His joy as your strength.

In the holy hush that sustains forever and a day

God Almighty grants his Beloved peace as they pray.

Excerpt from Give A Little Sunshine, Elizabeth Hilby ©2014

## *A Marriage Prayer*

Lord, I come humbly to your throne of grace. Break all pride, lack of forgiveness or offense off me in Jesus name. Help me to serve my spouse with a heart of love and respect. Lord, let there be less of me and more of you. I prefer ___ over myself and my needs. In Jesus name!

(wife) Help me to quiet my mouth Lord that ___ sees my chase, reverent behavior to draw him to yourself without any words (1 Peter 3:1). Lord, help me to respect and obey him as Christ; help him to love me as Christ loves the church (Ephesians 5:25).

Father give my husband/wife a discerning heart to know your gracious love and the great plans *You* have for our family. Plans to prosper and not to harm, to give us hope and a future. ___ is mighty in the kingdom of God fulfilling what you predestined for him/her to do. Every weapon formed against ___ will fail in Jesus name.

Father, I bind all word curses and release the Word of God over our life that does not fail. I pray we have the mind of Christ! Everything we set our hands to do will prosper in Jesus name. We are the head and not the tail. We have favor going in and coming out. Lord make us one as we are one with Jesus. Help me to love the way you love, unconditionally! Lord make our marriage all that you know it can be. Where change needs to take place, Lord, begin with me.

# Armor of God Test

Read each faith statement.
If you cannot agree, that is an area to work on with the
guidance of the Holy Spirit.

### The Helmet of Salvation

My eye gate is holy. I stand apart in my choices. I do
not blend in with the world. (Matthew 5:29-30)
I listen to music, jokes, and T.V. that are non-offensive
to Holy Spirit. (John 8:47, Luke 11:28)
My mouth speaks the Bible. (Luke 6:45, Proverbs
18:2)
My thoughts are Christ-focused. (Romans 12:2)

### Breastplate of Righteousness

My emotions are ruled by the Holy Spirit. (Philippians
4:7, Psalms 94:19)
My heart's desire is God. (Psalms 19, Matthew 5:8,
John 14:27, Colossians 3:1-3)
Saved by Grace means I am forgiven and forgiving.
(Matthew 6:14, Ephesians 2:8)
I am righteous, and nothing can separate me from
God's love! (Romans 8:38-39)

### Belt of Truth

To Satan, I am a target, but I know that He that is in
me is greater! (1 John 4:4, 1 Thessalonians 5:8)

### *Preparation of Peace guide my Feet*

I am a peace bearer. (Matthew 5:9, Romans 12:18, Romans 14:19)
I share the Good News. (Isaiah 52:7, 2 Corinthians 5:17-20)
I do greater works than Jesus because of his Holy Spirit in me. (John 14:12, Matthew 28:18-20)

### *Shield of Faith*

Faith rules me, not fear! (2 Samuel 22:36, Proverbs 18:10, Hebrews 11:1,6; 1 John 5:4, Ephesians 6:16)

Even if my faith falters, God is faithful to increase my faith to the level I need! (Luke 17:5, Mark 11:22-24)

### *Sword of the Spirit*

I win! I agree with God's vision of me. God says I am chosen, an heir of righteousness, forgiven, saved, appointed, free, a conqueror, sealed for His glory, healed, prosperous, one with Him, made in His image, the temple of the Holy Spirit, His Bride, Loved. (Hebrews 4:12, Matthew 4:4, Psalms 119:105, 2 Corinthians 10:4, Isaiah 55:11)

*Author, Elizabeth Hilby www.princesswriterllc.com/*

# *Healing Scriptures*

### *Renewed Mind:*

* Isaiah 53:1 Who has believed our report? To whom has the arm of the Lord been revealed? Declare: I believe God's report: by Jesus's stripes I am healed!

* Isaiah 26:3-4 I know You will keep me in perfect peace because my mind stays on You. I put my trust in You, Jesus. You are my everlasting strength.

* Proverbs 3:5-6 I will trust in the Lord with all my heart and lean not on my own understanding. In all my ways I acknowledge Him knowing He will direct my path.

* Matthew 11:29-30 Jesus, I take Your yoke as I learn from You. I know You are gentle and humble at heart. In You, I will have rest in my soul. Your yoke is easy and burdens light.

### *Trust:*

* 1 John 4:4 I am a child of God. I have overcome the world because He who is in me is greater than he who is in the world. Therefore, I am greater than the devil and all his principalities in this world. They will not have victory over me!

* Romans 8:27 "We know that He works all things out for good for those who love God and are called according to His purposes."

* Romans 8:37 We are conquerors in everything we see through Jesus who loves us and lives in us. Father, the battle is yours, but the victory is mine!

### *Healed:*

* Isaiah 53:5 The chastisement of my peace was upon Him, and by His stripes, I am healed.

* Philippians 2:9-11 "Therefore God has highly exalted Him and given Him the name which is above every name, that at the name of Jesus every knee shall bow, of those in heaven, and of those on earth, and of those under the earth, that every tongue should confess that Jesus Christ is Lord to the glory of the Father." (Declare the lack must bow to Jesus.)

* Revelations 12:11 I will overcome by the "Blood of the Lamb and the word of my testimony."

* Jeremiah 17:14 "Heal me O Lord and I shall be healed, save me O Lord and I shall be saved." I will live and declare the word of the Lord.

* Jeremiah 17:7-8 "Blessed is the man who trusts in the Lord, and whose hope is in the Lord. For he shall be like a tree planted by the waters. Which spreads out its roots by the river and will not fear when heat comes; but its leaf will be green and will not be anxious in the year of drought, nor will cease from yielding fruit."

*Author, Elizabeth Hilby www.princesswriterllc.com/*

## *Prayer for the Lost*

Lord break up the fallow ground of _____'s heart. Let your word and will be done in their life. Lord of the harvest, I pray as your word directs "Send the laborers* into the path of _____ in Jesus name. (*Hosea 10:1)

Father turn your heart to this your son/daughter and turn his/her heart to you! Malachi 4:6.

Father, it is not the will of man, but God that prospers in _____'s life. He/she will fulfill the call on their life written before he/she formed in his/her mother's womb.

Father overtake _____ with your goodness that draws a person to repentance. He/she will see the goodness of the Lord and turn to you in the land of the living. Romans 2:4

## *Prayer for Prosperity*

* Psalms 23:5 I thank you, Father, for the table you prepared for me in the presence of my enemies.


* Psalms 90:17 Father, may your favor rest on me. Establish the work of my hands to prosper in Jesus name.

* Psalms 84:11 Father, I thank you for favor and\honor. As I walk with your word, you do not withhold any good thing from me.

* Matthew 6:25-34 I know you provide for the sparrow and the lilies of the field I know you provide for me!

* Romans 14:17-18 "… but of righteousness, peace and joy in the Holy Spirit, because anyone who serves Christ in this way is pleasing to God and receives human approval." I thank you for righteousness, peace, and joy in the Holy Spirit. As I serve you, I have the favor of God from man on me to succeed.

Precious Life, Can I introduce you to my best friend? He is gentle and kind. He loves everyone. He wants to be your best friend too! His name is Jesus.

Don't turn away! He is here. He is standing at your heart's door knocking. If you invite him in, He will come. He brings with him peace, forgiveness, and hope. Things we all need. God sent Jesus, and He chose to be the sacrifice for the sins of all mankind. That includes you! He loves you more than life itself. He wants you to meet with him and let him clean and heal your broken heart. Because Jesus shed his blood for your sins, He can heal and save you!

If you want this, say this simple prayer, "Jesus, I am sorry I have sinned. Please forgive me; Come into my heart. I want you to be my Savior and Lord. I need you to be my friend. Amen" That is, it! You just entered the family of God.

I want to encourage you to go to a local church to grow in this relationship. Get a Bible or read one online every day, even if you do not understand it. The Spirit of God will teach you as you continue in faith to seek him. That's how we learn the character of Jesus. It is also how we learn to live in a way that pleases God the Father. You don't live right to get saved; you want to live right because you love God. Repentance means you turned from the sinfulness that had you in bondage and turned to the grace of Jesus to help you live holy.

You can also pray every day— any time, any place. You do that by merely talking to God like you do a friend. You do not have to be afraid to tell him anything! He already knows it all! Talking with him will also help you to build trust and a stronger relationship.

God bless and welcome to the family of God!

# *Journal Section*

This final section is for Journaling. Writing down what God does gives you a resource to refer back to in times of trouble. Make this your place of reverence and remembering what God has done or shows you he plans to do. Amen!

Then the LORD replied: "Write down the revelation

and make it plain on tablets

so that a herald may run with it.

For the revelation awaits an appointed time;

it speaks of the end

and will not prove false.

Though it linger,

Are You A Target?


wait for it.

It will certainly come

and will not delay." Habakkuk 2:2-3, NIV

## *Meet the Author*

Elizabeth (Liz) Hilby retired 2014 after 23 years as a para-educator for special needs children to become a full-time grandmother and writer. She earned her degree in Christian Counseling in 2019; has a column in the LA Road Trip magazine, leads a Life Group, and does community teaching.

Liz believes, if you hear and obey God, you can enjoy an incredible partnership and journey with him. That is what she has done in writing from her faith to inspire others in theirs for God's glory! Her hoped for achievement in writing is to deepen Christian faith and equip brothers and sisters in the Lord for the battles of life.

Liz entered a new genre' in 2018. She hopes to inspire children with entertaining stories and Bible Studies through children's books. As with her adult books, she teaches godly morals and includes interactive question. Liz may be contacted at:

www.princesswriterllc.com or eghilby@yahoo.com

**Liz's books to date include:**

*Self-published books include:*

*Give A Little Sunshine: Sentiments for Cards and Scrapbooks*

*31 Days At The Cross,* Daily Devotions

*A B C Santa & Me Activity book*

*Pear River Santa Coloring book*

Available through Amazon.com, Barnes & Noble.com, author's website, and local bookstores.

———

*Published by Traditional publisher Pen It! Publications, LLC*

*Are You a Target? Fight the Good Fight God's Way*

*Exploring God's Word Together Bible Study for Adults and Little Ones (2 Book Set)*

*Red Owl Learns Jesus Loves Me*

*Red Owl's Cup of Strawberries (story and song)*

Available online at **www.penitpublications.com bookstore,** Amazon, Barnes & Noble, and locally.

Please consider writing a review where you purchase. Reviews help my books be discovered.

*May God bless you and yours with the abundance of his love and grace.*

And remember,

*Victory is yours because Jesus already won the war!*

*From bent knees, Liz*

www.ingramcontent.com/pod-product-compliance
Lightning Source LLC
Chambersburg PA
CBHW072043040426
42447CB00012BB/2996